HOUGHTON MIFFLIN
Soar to Success

Student Guide
Level 3

Authors
David Chard
J. David Cooper

 HOUGHTON MIFFLIN   BOSTON

Printed in U.S.A.

ISBN-13: 978-0-618-940820
ISBN-10: 0-618-94082-0

456789-VH-13 12 11 10 09 08

Name _____

Reflection

1 Which facts about eggs and tadpoles did you find most interesting? Why?

_____

_____

_____

_____

_____

Name _____

2 Summarize what you learned about how tadpoles eat.

_____
_____
_____
_____
_____
_____

Name _____

Reflection
••••••••••

 Circle the strategy you used most.

Strategy Box			
Predict	Clarify	Question	Summarize

Name at least one place where you used this strategy. Write the page number(s).

_____

_____

_____

How did this strategy help you?

_____

_____

_____

_____

Name _____

Reflection

1 How do you think Melanie and Grandpa felt after Arthur "helped" them? Explain why.

_____

_____

_____

_____

Reflection

2 Do you think Arthur should be rewarded richly when he does a task properly? _____ Why or why not?

_____

_____

_____

_____

_____

_____

_____

_____

Name _____

Reflection

  Circle the strategy you used most.

Strategy Box			
Predict	Clarify	Question	Summarize

_____

_____

_____

_____

How did this strategy help you?

_____

_____

_____

_____

_____

_____

Wild Bears

Name _____

1 How might a bear be dangerous to another animal?

_____

_____

_____

_____

_____

Reflection

2 Summarize what happens when a bear hibernates.

_____

_____

_____

_____

_____

Name _____

Reflection
....

3 What kind of bear would you like to learn more about?
What would you like to know?

_____

_____

_____

_____

_____

Name _____

Reflection

Circle the section you liked best in *Wild Bears*.

Pages 4–9

Bears live all over the world. They come in different sizes and colors. They have strong bodies and are fast runners.

Pages 10–17

Bears have poor eyesight but good senses of hearing and smell. Bears hibernate in the winter. Bears have cubs. Cubs spend up to three years with their mother.

Pages 18–25

Facts about brown bears, black bears, polar bears, and sun bears

Pages 26–32

Facts about sloth bears, spectacled bears, and panda bears

Circle the strategy you found most helpful while reading *Wild Bears*.

Strategy Box			
Predict	Clarify	Question	Summarize

The _____ strategy helped me read

pages _____ because _____

_____

_____

_____

Arturo's Baton

Name _____

Reflection
● ● ● ● ● ● ● ● ●

1 Why do you think Arturo likes to conduct the orchestra?

_____

_____

_____

_____

Reflection
● ● ● ● ● ● ● ● ●

2 Do you think Arturo should cancel the next concert and tour? Why?

_____

_____

_____

_____

Name _____

 Circle the strategy you used most.

Strategy Box			
Predict	Clarify	Question	Summarize

Name one place in the story where you used this strategy.

_____

_____

_____

Explain how this strategy helped.

_____

_____

_____

_____

_____

Name _____

Reflection
• • • • • • • • •

4 What did Arturo learn when he conducted
without his baton?

_____

_____

_____

_____

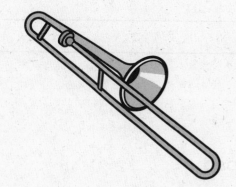

Name _____

Reflection

1 How is the way that a penguin uses its wings different from the way most birds use their wings?

_____

_____

_____

_____

_____

_____

_____

_____

Name _____

Reflection
• • • • • • • • •

2 If you see an Emperor penguin on land, what does that tell you?

_____

_____

_____

_____

_____

_____

_____

Name _____

Reflection

3 List at least four facts that you learned about Emperor penguins. Circle the fact that you find most interesting. Then explain why you think as you do.

_____

_____

_____

_____

_____

_____

I think this fact is interesting because

_____

_____

_____

_____

Name _____

Reflection

What do you like to do more than anything else in the world?

_____

_____

_____

_____

Reflection

2 Why does the wolf decide not to catch the chicken right away?

_____

_____

_____

_____

Name _____

Reflection

3 What would you do with all the food that the wolf bakes?

_____

_____

_____

_____

_____

Name _____

Reflection

Circle the strategy you used most in the story.

Strategy Box

Predict	Clarify	Question	Summarize

On what page(s) did you use this strategy?

_____

_____

_____

How did this strategy help you?

_____

_____

_____

Name _____

1 Was it right for Harry to bring home the wounded bird? Why do you think so?

_____

_____

_____

_____

_____

2 Why do the birds follow Harry and stay outside his window?

_____

_____

_____

_____

_____

Name _____

Reflection
• • • • • • • •

Circle the strategy you used most in this lesson.

Strategy Box			
Predict	Clarify	Question	Summarize

Where did you use this strategy?

_____

How did this strategy help you?

_____

_____

_____

_____

_____

_____

Name _____

4 What did you like best about the story?

_____

_____

_____

_____

_____

_____

Why?

_____

_____

_____

_____

_____

BIRD
SEED

Name _____

K-W-L Chart

Title	

What I **K**now	What I **W**ant to Find Out	What I **L**earned
	Pages 2–10	**Pages 2–10**
	Pages 11–20	**Pages 11–20**
	Pages 21–32	**Pages 21–32**

Name _____

Reflection

Think about the ways that an octopus, a bombardier beetle, a puffer fish, and a glass snake escape enemies. What do they all have in common?

_____

_____

_____

_____

_____

Reflection

Which animal that you have read about so far would you most like to watch as it protects itself? Explain reasons for your choice.

_____

_____

_____

_____

_____

_____

Name _____

Circle the section you liked best in *What Do You Do When Something Wants to Eat You?*

Pages 2–10

Many animals are in constant danger. They find ways to protect themselves. The octopus shoots ink. The bombardier beetle shoots out hot chemicals.

Pages 11–20

A pangolin rolls up into an armor-plated ball. The lizard walks on water. The hog-nosed snake plays dead. A hover fly looks like a stinging wasp.

Pages 21–32

The frog glides between the trees. The silkmoth reveals eye markings. The skink wiggles a blue tongue.

Name _____

Reflection
● ● ● ● ● ● ● ●

1 What does migrate mean?

_____

_____

_____

_____

_____

_____

Reflection
● ● ● ● ● ● ● ●

2 Summarize how a woodchuck gets ready for winter.

_____

_____

_____

_____

_____

_____

Name _____

Reflection
••••••••

3 Why do pikas cut more grass than they can eat in the summer?

_____

_____

_____

_____

_____

Reflection
••••••••

4 What animal interests you most in this book? Why?

_____

_____

_____

_____

_____

_____

Name _____

Reflection

Circle a strategy that helped you read this book.

Strategy Box

Predict	Clarify	Question

Find a place in the book where you used this strategy.

I used this strategy on page(s) _____

Tell how you used the strategy.

_____

_____

_____

_____

_____

_____

Name _____

Story Map

Title

Setting

Characters

Problem

Major Events

Outcome

Name _____

Reflection

1 What is another way the stranger might pay for his meal?

_____

_____

_____

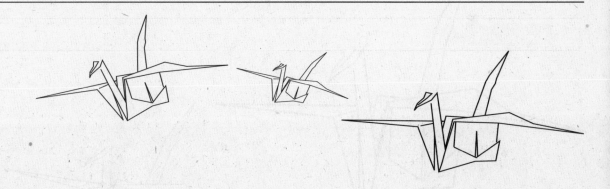

Reflection

2 Why would a dancing crane make people want to come to a restaurant?

_____

_____

_____

_____

_____

_____

_____

_____

Name _____

3 Would you like to eat a meal in this restaurant? Why or
why not?

_____

_____

_____

_____

_____

_____

Name _____

Reflection
••••••••••

 Circle the strategy you used most.

Strategy Box			
Predict	Clarify	Question	Summarize

Name at least one place where you used this strategy or modeled it for someone else. Write the page number(s).

_____

How did this strategy help you?

_____

_____

_____

_____

Name _____

Reflection

1 How are whales different from fish?

_____

_____

_____

_____

_____

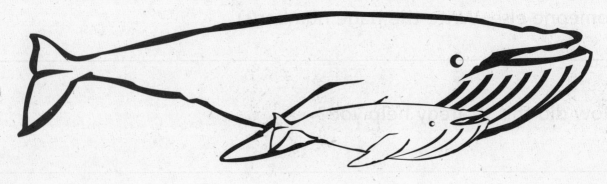

Reflection

2 Summarize how a whale breathes.

_____

_____

_____

_____

Name _____

Reflection
••••••••••

3 What kinds of sounds do whales make?

_____

_____

_____

_____

Why do you think they make these sounds?

_____

_____

_____

_____

_____

_____

_____

_____

Name _____

Reflection

Circle the section you liked best in *Baby Whales Drink Milk.*

Pages 4–9 Whales are mammals.	**Pages 10–17** Newborn whales
Pages 18–23 **Whales' temperature, blubber, and sounds**	**Pages 24–32** Where whales live, what they eat

How did one of the four strategies help you read that section?

Predict

_____

_____

Clarify

_____

_____

Question

_____

_____

Summarize

_____

_____

Name _____

Story Map

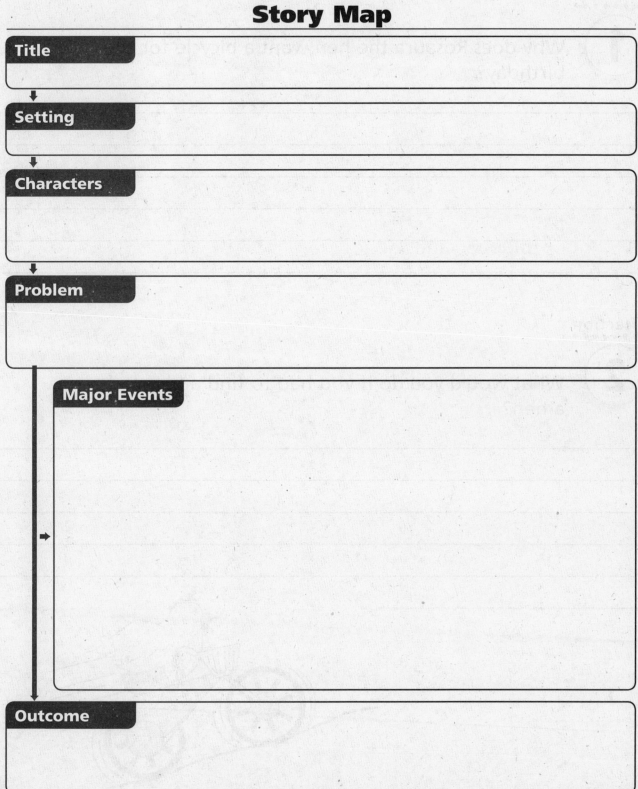

Title

Setting

Characters

Problem

Major Events

Outcome

Name _____

Reflection

Why does Rosaura the hen want a bicycle for her birthday?

_____

_____

_____

_____

_____

Reflection

What would you do if you had to find a bicycle for a hen?

_____

_____

_____

_____

_____

Name _____

Reflection

3 What seems strange about the man who comes to the town?

_____

_____

_____

_____

_____

_____

_____

Name _____

Reflection

 4 Circle the strategy you used most.

Strategy Box			
Predict	Clarify	Question	Summarize

Name at least one place where you used this strategy or modeled it for someone else. Write the page number(s). _____

How did this strategy help you?

_____

_____

_____

_____

_____

Name _____

· · · · · · · ·

1 Why do you think the bald eagle was chosen as a symbol of our country?

_____

_____

_____

_____

_____

_____

_____

_____

· · · · · · · ·

2 Summarize how the bald eagle catches its prey.

_____

_____

_____

_____

_____

_____

_____

_____

Reflection

Circle the strategy you used most.

Strategy Box			
Predict	Clarify	Question	Summarize

On what page(s) did you use this strategy?

I used the _____ strategy on page(s)_____.

How did this strategy help you?

_____

_____

_____

_____

Name _____

Reflection

4 Why should people not get too close to a bald eagle's nest?

_____

_____

_____

_____

_____

Reflection

5 What can people do to help bald eagles?

_____

_____

_____

_____

Name _____

Story Map

Title

Setting

Characters

Problem

Major Events

Outcome

Name _____

Reflection

1 Do you think a fish makes a good pet? Why or why not?

_____

_____

_____

_____

_____

_____

Reflection

2 Do you think the boy is changing his mind about Norman? Why or why not?

_____

_____

_____

_____

_____

_____

_____

Reflection

3 How do you think Norman feels about being the boy's pet? What clues make you think so?

_____

_____

_____

_____

_____

_____

Name _____

Reflection
• • • • • • • • •

Circle the strategy you found most helpful while reading *Not Norman: A Goldfish Story.*

Strategy Box			
Predict	Clarify	Question	Summarize

Name at least one place where you used this strategy or modeled it for someone else. Write the page number(s).

_____

_____

_____

How did this strategy help you?

_____

_____

_____

_____

_____

_____

_____

Name _____

Reflection

1 How are the pitcher plant and the Venus flytrap alike? How are they different?

_____

_____

_____

_____

Reflection

2 If foxglove is used to make medicine, then why is it dangerous for people to eat the plant?

_____

_____

_____

_____

_____

_____

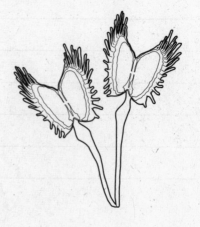

Name _____

 Which fact about plants that you have read so far do you find most interesting? Explain reasons for your choice.

_____

_____

_____

_____

_____

_____

Name _____

Reflection

Circle the strategy you found most helpful while reading *Weird and Wacky Plants*

Strategy Box			
Predict	Clarify	Question	Summarize

Name at least one place where you used this strategy or modeled it for someone else. Write the page number(s).

_____

_____

How did this strategy help you?

_____

_____

_____

_____

_____

_____

Name _____

K-W-L Chart

Title

What I **K**now	What I **W**ant to Find Out	What I **L**earned

Name _____

Reflection

Are you afraid of snakes? Explain why or why not.

_____
_____
_____
_____
_____

Reflection

What is unusual about the way giant snakes eat?

_____
_____
_____
_____
_____

Name _____

(3) Which fact about anacondas do you find most interesting? Explain reasons for your choice.

_____

_____

_____

_____

_____

(4) How is a python different from a boa?

_____

_____

_____

_____

_____

_____

_____

Name _____

Reflection

Circle the strategy you found most helpful while reading *Giant Snakes.*

Strategy Box			
Predict	Clarify	Question	Summarize

Name at least one place where you used this strategy or modeled it for someone else. Write the page number(s).

_____

How did this strategy help you?

_____

_____

_____

_____

_____

Name _____

Reflection

(1) What is waste?

_____
_____
_____
_____

Reflection

(2) Summarize what happens to waste at a landfill.

_____
_____
_____
_____
_____

Name _____

Reflection

 Circle the strategy you used most.

Strategy Box			
Predict	Clarify	Question	Summarize

Where did you use this strategy or model it for someone else?

I used the _____ strategy on

pages(s) _____ .

How did this strategy help you?

The _____ strategy helped me

_____

_____

_____

_____

Name _____

Reflection
• • • • • • • •

4 What household items do you use that might be made from recycled materials?

_____

_____

_____

_____

_____

Reflection
• • • • • • • •

5 Why do you think the author wrote this book?

_____

_____

_____

_____

_____

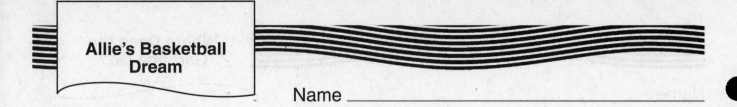

Story Map

Title

Setting

Characters

Problem

Major Events

Outcome

Name _____

Reflection

Why did the boys laugh at Allie when she tried to play basketball?

_____
_____
_____
_____
_____
_____

Reflection

Would you respond to Allie's friends in the same way she did? Why or why not?

_____
_____
_____

Name _____

Reflection

3 What does Allie tell Buddy about girls playing basketball?

_____
_____
_____
_____
_____
_____
_____
_____
_____

Name _____

Reflection

Circle the chapter you like best in *Allie's Basketball Dream*.

Pages 2–9 Allie gets the basketball and begins to play	**Pages 10–17** Allie's friends won't play with her.
Pages 18–23 Buddy tries to trade with Allie.	**Pages 24–30** Allie begins to make baskets.

Choose a strategy that helped you read that section. Then explain how the strategy helped you.

Strategy Box

Predict	Clarify	Question	Summarize

The _____ strategy helped me read

pages _____ because

_____

_____

_____

Name _____

Reflection

1 What things do Sam and Jackson do that show you that they are very interested in baseball? What interests you in this same way? What do you do that shows people your interest?

_____

_____

_____

_____

_____

Reflection

2 How can you tell that Sam is a very good friend to Jackson?

_____

_____

_____

_____

_____

_____

Name _____

Reflection

3   How is it working out for Jackson to be the peanut vendor? Do you think it was a good idea? Why or why not?

_____

_____

_____

_____

_____

_____

_____

_____

_____

_____

_____

_____

_____

_____

_____

_____

_____

_____

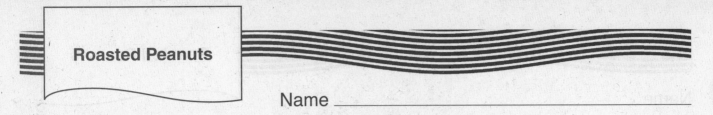

Name _____

Circle the strategy you found most helpful while reading
Roasted Peanuts.

Strategy Box			
Predict	Clarify	Question	Summarize

Name at least one place where you used this strategy or
modeled it for someone else. Write the page number(s).

_____

_____

_____

How did this strategy help you?

_____

_____

_____

_____

_____

_____

_____

Name _____

Semantic Map

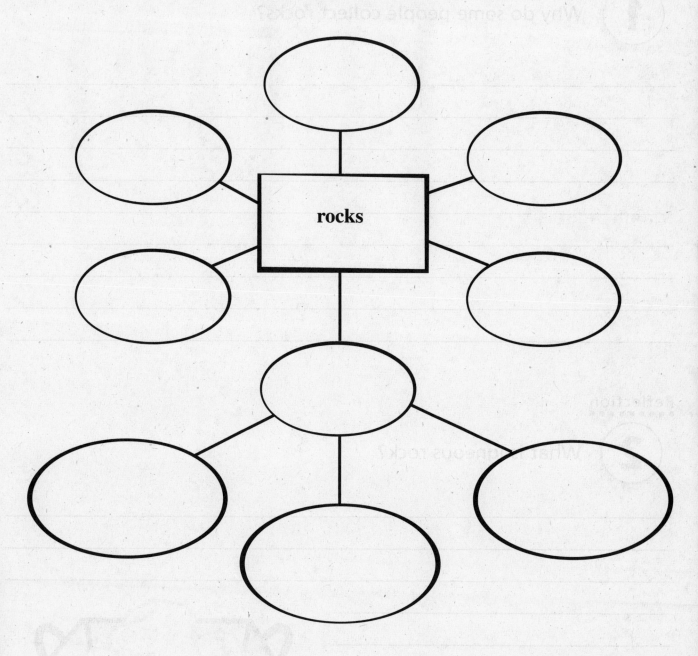

rocks

Let's Go Rock Collecting

Name _____

1 Why do some people collect rocks?

_____

_____

_____

_____

_____

_____

_____

_____

2 What is igneous rock?

_____

_____

_____

_____

_____

_____

Name _____

Reflection

 3   Circle the strategy you used most.

Strategy Box			
Predict	Clarify	Question	Summarize

Name at least one place where you used this strategy or modeled it for someone else. Write the page number(s).

_____

How did this strategy help you?

_____

_____

_____

_____

_____

_____

Name _____

Reflection

4 How does shale change into slate?

_____
_____
_____
_____
_____
_____

Reflection

5 What kinds of things would you like to collect? Why?

_____
_____
_____
_____
_____
_____
_____

Story Map

Name _____

Title

Setting

Characters

Problem

Major Events

Outcome

Name _____

Reflection
• • • • • • • • •

1 Why do you think Marisol wants to have a dog?

_____

_____

_____

_____

_____

_____

_____

Reflection
• • • • • • • • •

2 Why does Pancho stay near Marisol's house?

_____

_____

_____

_____

_____

_____

_____

Name _____

Reflection
· · · · · · · · ·

3 Why is Marisol worried about Pancho?

_____

_____

_____

_____

_____

_____

_____

What would you do if you were Marisol?

_____

_____

_____

_____

_____

_____

_____

Name _____

Reflection
••••••••••

Circle the chapter you like best in *The Outside Dog*.

Chapter 1	**Chapter 2**
Marisol Wants a Dog	A Collar for Pancho
Chapter 3	**Chapter 4**
The Search	Pancho Saves the Day

Circle a strategy that helped you read that chapter.

Strategy Box

Predict	Clarify	Question	Summarize

I used the _____ strategy to help me

_____

_____

_____

_____

Name _____

Reflection
••••••••••

1 Why do Susan and Sarah love going to Aunt Flossie's house?

_____

_____

_____

_____

Reflection
••••••••••

2 What does Aunt Flossie remember about the big Baltimore fire?

_____

_____

_____

_____

_____

Name _____

Reflection

3 Why does Aunt Flossie have a story for every one of her hats?

_____

_____

_____

_____

_____

_____

Reflection

4 Which of Aunt Flossie's stories do you like best?

_____

_____

_____

Why do you like this story?

_____

_____

_____

_____

Name _____

Reflection

5 Circle the section you liked best in *Aunt Flossie's Hats (and Crab Cakes Later).*

The smoky
green hat

The blue hat with
a red feather

The favorite
Sunday straw hat

How did one or more of the four strategies help you read that section?

Predict _____

_____

Clarify _____

_____

Question _____

_____

_____

Summarize _____

_____

Name _____

K-W-L Chart

Title

What I **K**now	What I **W**ant to Find Out	What I **L**earned

Name _____

My Notes to Clarify

Write any words or ideas that you need to clarify. Include the page numbers.

Words or Ideas	Page
Pages 4–13	
Pages 14–17	
Pages 18–21	
Pages 22–27	
Pages 22–27	

Name _____

Reflection

1   What is the fish fossil made of?

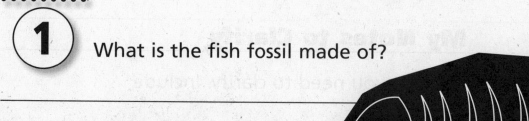

_____

_____

_____

_____

_____

_____

_____

_____

Reflection

2   Summarize how a dinosaur's footprint becomes a fossil.

_____

_____

_____

_____

_____

_____

_____

_____

_____

Name _____

Reflection
• • • • • • • •

3 Circle the section you liked best so far in *Fossils Tell of Long Ago*

Fossils of bones

Fossils in ice and amber

Fossils of imprints

How did one or more of the four strategies help you read that section?

Predict _____

_____

Summarize _____

_____

Clarify _____

_____

Question _____

_____

_____

Name _____

Reflection

4 What can people learn from fossils?

_____

_____

_____

_____

_____

_____

_____

Reflection

5 What kind of fossil would you like to find? What would you like to learn from it?

_____

_____

_____

_____

_____

_____

_____

_____

Name _____

My Notes to Clarify

Write any words or ideas that you need to clarify. Include the page numbers.

Words or Ideas	Page
Pages 2–9	
Pages 10–15	
Pages 16–21	
Pages 22–30	

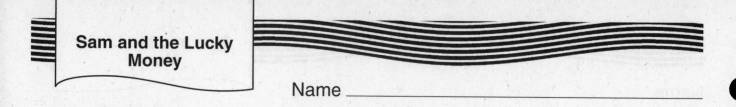

Name _____

Story Map

Title

Setting

Characters

Problem

Major Events

Outcome

Name _____

Reflection

1 How do you think Sam feels when he sees the old man with bare feet?

_____

_____

_____

_____

_____

_____

_____

Reflection

2 Why doesn't Sam buy any sweets in the bakery?

_____

_____

_____

_____

_____

_____

Name _____

Reflection

3 Why does Sam feel angry in the toy store?

_____

_____

_____

_____

_____

How would you feel?

_____

_____

_____

_____

_____

Name _____

Circle the section you liked best in *Sam and the Lucky Money.*

Pages 2–9 Sam discovers the barefoot man.	**Pages 10–15** Sam sees the lion.
Pages 16–21 Sam gets angry.	**Pages 22–30** Sam gives money to the barefoot man.

How did one or more of the four strategies help you read that section?

Predict _____

_____

Clarify _____

_____

Question _____

_____

Summarize _____

_____

_____

Name _____

My Notes to Clarify

Write any words or ideas that you need to clarify. Include the page numbers.

Words or Ideas	Page
Pages 1–16	
Pages 17–29	
Pages 30–40	
What happened to Michael's soup?	
Pages 41–56	

Name _____

Story Map

Title	

Setting	

Characters	

Problem	

Major Events	

Outcome	

Name _____

Reflection

1 Did what Michael expected about his new name happen? Explain.

_____
_____
_____
_____
_____
_____
_____
_____
_____
_____
_____
_____
_____
_____
_____
_____

Name _____

Reflection

2 What do you think about the way that Michael is trying to handle his problem? Do you think it will work over time? Why or why not?

_____

_____

_____

_____

_____

_____

_____

_____

_____

_____

_____

_____

_____

_____

_____

_____

_____

_____

Name _____

Reflection
••••••••••

3 What would you do if you were in Michael's position?

_____

_____

_____

_____

_____

_____

_____

_____

_____

_____

_____

_____

_____

_____

_____

_____

_____

_____

_____

_____

_____

Name _____

Reflection
••••••••••

Circle the strategy you found most helpful while reading *Just Like Mike*.

Strategy Box			
Predict	Clarify	Question	Summarize

Name at least one place where you used this strategy or modeled it for someone else. Write the page number(s).

_____

_____

How did this strategy help you?

_____

_____

_____

_____

_____

_____

Name _____

My Notes to Clarify

Write any words or ideas that you need to clarify. Include the page numbers.

Words or Ideas	Page
Pages 3–9	
Pages 10–21	
Pages 22–29	
Pages 30–39	
Pages 40–46	

Name _____

Event Map

Title

↓

Event 1

↓

Event 2

↓

Event 3

↓

Event 4

↓

Event 5

Name _____

Reflection
••••••••

1 What did the children think about the cloud that they saw coming on the prairie?

_____

_____

_____

_____

_____

Reflection
••••••••

2 Why was it so important for the Lundstroms to get rid of the grasshoppers?

_____

_____

_____

_____

_____

Name _____

Reflection
● ● ● ● ● ● ● ● ●

3 Circle the strategy you used most so far.

Strategy Box			
Predict	Clarify	Question	Summarize

Name at least one place where you used this strategy or modeled it for someone else. Write the page number(s).

_____

_____

_____

How did this strategy help you?

_____

_____

_____

Name _____

4 Why did Mr. Lundstrom leave to work at the lumber camp?

_____

_____

_____

_____

_____

Reflection

5 Do you think the Lundstrom family will continue to be able to survive on the prairie?

_____

_____

_____

_____

_____

Name _____

My Notes to Clarify

Write any words or ideas that you need to clarify. Include the page numbers.

Words or Ideas	Page
Pages 1–10	
Pages 11–21	
Pages 22–28	
Pages 29–38	
Pages 39–44	

Name _____

Event Map

Title

Event 1

Event 2

Event 3

Event 4

Event 5

Event 6

Event 7

Name _____

Reflection
● ● ● ● ● ● ● ● ●

1 Why do you think that Jeff is so determined to find a jaguar?

_____

_____

_____

_____

_____

_____

_____

Reflection
● ● ● ● ● ● ● ● ●

2 Name at least two things that Jeff has learned while being in the rain forest.

_____

_____

_____

_____

_____

_____

Name _____

Reflection

(3) Would you like to go on a research trip like the one Jeff is on? Why or why not?

_____

_____

_____

_____

_____

_____

Name _____

Reflection

 Was it wise for Jeff to chase the butterfly into the jungle alone? Explain why you think as you do.

_____

_____

_____

_____

_____

_____

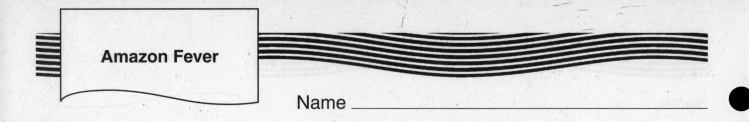

Name _____

Reflection

 Circle the strategy you found most helpful while reading *Amazon Fever.*

Strategy Box			
Predict	Clarify	Question	Summarize

Name at least one place where you used this strategy or modeled it for someone else. Write the page number(s).

_____

_____

How did this strategy help you?

_____

_____

_____

_____

_____

Name _____

My Notes to Clarify

Write any words or ideas that you need to clarify. Include the page numbers.

Words or Ideas	Page
Pages 1–11	
Pages 12–21	
Pages 22–30	
Pages 31–42	

Name _____

Story Map

Title

Setting

Characters

Problem

Major Events

Outcome

Name _____

Reflection

1 Do you think Billy Wade put the snake in the flour bin? Why or why not?

_____
_____
_____
_____
_____
_____

Reflection

2 Why did Kate believe the snake was in the flour bin long enough to get warm?

_____
_____
_____
_____
_____
_____
_____
_____
_____

Name _____

Reflection

3 Do you think Mickey and Kate are good detectives? Why or why not?

_____

_____

_____

_____

_____

_____

Would you like to be a detective? Why or why not?

_____

_____

_____

_____

_____

_____

_____

Name _____

Reflection

Circle the section you liked best in *The April Fool's Day Mystery*.

Chapters 1-2 "Puzzles and Pranks" and "A Real Private Eye"	**Chapters 3-5** "Sleuthing Snakes" to "Caught in the Library"
Chapters 6–7 "The scene of the Crime" and "What Mr. Butterfield Knows"	**Chapters 8–10** "What Suzy Didn't Know" to "The Case is Closed"

How did one or more of the four strategies help you read that section?

Predict _____

_____

Clarify _____

_____

Summarize _____

_____

Question _____

_____

Name _____

Clarify/Phonics How to Say a Word

When I come to a word I don't know, first I look for chunks I know.

I know _____. If I still don't know the word, I look for letter

sounds. In this word, I know the sounds _____, _____, and _____.

If I blend the sounds together, the word is _____.

Finally, I check the meaning by rereading the sentence.

Clarify A Word Meaning

I read this word: _____. I'm not sure what

this word is or what it means. I look at the picture or read

to the end of the sentence. Now I think the word means . . .

Clarify An Idea

I don't understand this idea: _____.

First I _____ (reread, look at pictures, etc.). Then

I understand that....I reread the sentence and it makes sense.

Name _____

Predict

When I predict, I use clues from the pictures or from what I have read to help me figure out what will happen next (or what I will learn). I predict...

Question

When I question, I ask something that can be answered as I read or after I finish reading. I might ask . . .

Summarize

When I summarize, I tell in my own words the important things I have read.

Book Log

Title	Author	Date Completed	Comments

Name _____

Book Log

Title	Author	Date Completed	Comments